# How To Save Your Relationship:

## Find Out Proven Ways to Save Your Relationship and Marriage

Katherina C. Norton

Table of Contents

# Chapter 1

Over the last several years, there has been much discussion and disagreement over the figure that 50% of marriages end in divorce, yet the percentage keeps changing. The choice of whether or whether to get married is often delayed for younger generations. Although the divorce rate varies based on demographics, it may happen to any relationship, and most couples have very serious anxiety about avoiding a permanent breakup. Here are some other reasons that go unmentioned for divorce, even though money and communication are two of the most frequent reasons.

01 Insufficient Investment

We consider investments in terms of monetary value. We overlook the fact that learning how to sustain good relationships requires both time and knowledge commitment. "Why do we believe that entering a marriage doesn't need any special skills? What other position would we accept without any training? For example, giving your spouse two to three hours of your undivided attention each day. You should also seek out couples therapy and/or read books to assist you to deal with the challenges of marriage.

02. Unforgiveness

One of the main causes of marriages failing is our unwillingness to fully forgive our spouses. Couples find it extremely challenging to forgive since it requires us to treat our partners as if the incident never occurred. We repeatedly go through the traumatic events from the past, which prevents the wounds from ever being able to heal.

03 Missing Your Spouse's Appointment

A marriage might experience a lot of different things. It's crucial for our partners to "show up" at some of the most trying times in our lives, such as when we lose our homes, children pass away, or parents get ill. Instead of assuming what your spouse needs, Sadler advocates being able to question, "What is it that you need?" She mentions the inclination we have to just want to solve the problem as a huge problem. Not every circumstance has to be resolved. Sadler cautions that sometimes all you need to do is turn up. Finding the opportunity to speak through these challenging circumstances and be honest with your partner while also being able to convey that you may have but may not know what you need at the moment is part of showing up.

04 Ignoring the Relationship

We've never encountered the pressure that comes with the labels "husband" and "wife" in our relationships before getting married.

Without realizing it, we often go so far away from the bond that was forged throughout the courting phase after the wedding. Sadler suggests that we approach marriage with friendship at the fore and learn to speak to our spouses from a friend's viewpoint without being always so easily upset.

## 05 Unstated Preferences

This is a very precise piece of the jigsaw that is sometimes overlooked, but it is undoubtedly one that permeates our capacity to communicate. We don't only miss the chance to express our expectations; we also start acting as if they weren't fulfilled. "We come from diverse backgrounds and have different expectations, but we never express it to our partners. Men never really understand how important security is to women. Although it's something we believe guys should be aware of, it's seldom covered in depth. Men are being raised in homes with just one parent, and they lack role models.

06. Lack of Flexibility

"Even if a couple has done their homework and spoken about and comes to an understanding on the important issues, including economics and parenting styles, there has to be flexibility in the plans. After a kid joins the family, a partner's views on working outside the house may alter, or health problems may develop that affect your sexual connection. "I believe that the key to handling unexpected changes is to keep in mind that you and your spouse are on the same team and should work together to solve the problem rather than competing with one another. Making an appointment with a couple's therapist may be a fantastic method to assist you both get some clarity and perspective if you find it tough to accomplish this on your own.

07. Societal pressure or familial pressure

Our families often have opinions on whom we should marry. To avoid receiving the stigma of being "30-something and unmarried," women often race against time to find a partner and have a family. This, according to certain beliefs, might result in hasty marital choices that can ultimately result in divorce. the pressure that women experience while considering marriage. People may eventually realize the risks of living and loving others, and as a result, they may decide to end their marriage. In such a situation, it could be the wisest choice for everybody concerned. Finding yourself is never too late, and most of us need to do it periodically.

08 Lack of Self-Awareness

"There are a variety of individuals who have never considered what they enjoy or need, as well as others who follow what their families believe is best for them. They date persons who seem attractive on paper for the sake of the family and the public perception. It depends on the person and their life experiences whether this is done to blend in or stick out. "My suggestion is to spend your time getting to know and love yourself to overcome this. Recognize your likes and dislikes. Keep track of your emotions in different circumstances and whether you can get through them fast or not. So that you don't internalize your emotions, discuss them with your spouse, your friends, or a therapist. Finally, acknowledge that you will evolve. It's acceptable if what you enjoy at 25 is different from what you like at 30.

09 Failing to divide up parental responsibilities

There is much pleasure in raising children, but there is also a lot of effort and expense involved. Determining which parents will ensure that the kid is nourished, attends school, develops a moral sense, enjoys good social connections, and much more requires constant contact. Parents must regularly participate in school activities, check their kids' assignments, respond to their queries, and much more. The duty for parenting and discipline should fall on both parents.

Resentments might develop when one parent believes the other isn't contributing enough. Frustrations may persist. If a parent feels that divorce is the only option to compel a resolution when the child's needs aren't being addressed, they may be right.

10 Ignoring issues rather than talking about them

Relationships need everyday judgments regarding several matters, such as what to do for the day's activities and what duties need to be completed. Marriage involves making long-term choices, such as what each partner wants for their work. Couples must make the time to listen to each other's worries and address them honestly. When issues are left unresolved for too long, one partner may believe that communication is impossible.

11 A lackluster sexual life

Communication may help with certain sexual issues. But often, the romance and intimacy that formerly existed in the marriage are gone. There is no longer a yearning for intimacy. Many partners determine that the marriage should terminate when the fire just isn't burning.

spouses who make fresh connections or renew old ones

A significant marital contract violation occurs when a spouse gets back together with an ex-girlfriend or ex-boyfriend or becomes intimate with someone who is not their spouse. Some couples can accept having a second relationship. Many pairs are unable. The hurt spouse believes they are left with no alternative but to file for divorce and employ a family lawyer.

12 Budgetary issues

Financial difficulties are another factor that is not included in the Huffington Post stories. When one partner is working and the other isn't, the working partner may feel pressure to dissolve the union. A spouse who forgoes a profession to raise the kids could feel taken advantage of. Even when both partners are employed, there are sometimes insufficient funds to cover all of the expenses. One spouse's expensive addiction or inability to manage money might also lead a marriage to dissolve.

There are several other causes of divorce. Whatever the cause, a spouse who is dissatisfied with the marriage should get advice from a reputable Sevierville attorney who can lay out your alternatives and help you choose your priorities. Our attorneys at Adrian H. Altshuler & Associates assist clients in navigating these distressing times. You and your children's needs may be met by speaking with a divorce attorney.

# Chapter 2

Merriam Webster Dictionary defines a friend as "a person you like and like being with," while a best friend is described as "one's closest and dearest friend." Friends have the same interests, and the closest among them even experience life's pleasures and tragedies together. One of the many advantages of marriage might be that your spouse can become your closest friend. It's excellent if you and your husband are already close friends; if not, it may be time to realize how crucial friendship is to a happy marriage.

One of the traits of a successful and long-lasting marriage as well as the cornerstone of a happy marriage is friendship. According to research, happy marriages are more likely to have wonderful friendships between partners. It's believed that married couples' emotional bond is five times more significant than their level of physical closeness. Friendship-based relationships enjoy their time together and are truly attracted to one another. Because they have their favorite person to spend their lives with, their hobbies and interests are improved.

Marriages may be strengthened by fostering their marital friendship, which is believed to increase emotional and physical closeness. Friendship enables married people to feel confident enough to communicate more honestly with one another without fear of rejection or insecurity. Marriage requires experience, patience, and work to nurture and develop that connection. The skills and practices listed here can help you maintain and enhance your marriage.

Building Marital Friendships:

Time: Invest time in your relationship.
Talk and share about your daily life while communicating.
Trust: Be sincere and devoted.
Discover shared interests. Take pleasure in one another. As a group, laugh create enduring memories Together and attempt new things.
Objectives: Together, set and work toward your own goals. dream together
Make your partner feel important by placing them first. Respect one another and treat one other fairly. Celebrate each other's accomplishments When in need, rely on one another. Respect your partner Take care of one another. Be kind to one another and don't harbor resentments.
Being best friends with your partner or maintaining that friendship depends on how well you know each other. Get to know you or "self trivia" games may be a beneficial and enjoyable activity. Test each other's knowledge of specifics like your blood type, favorite music, and greatest turn-on. Make

the reward something like who cleans the home, who gives foot or back massages, or who gets to choose the winner's favorite movie or eatery.

In a marriage, emotional closeness may not last as long as physical intimacy does. True friendship last forever. A Marriage and Family Therapist may assist if you and your spouse are having trouble developing or maintaining your friendship.

Emotional intimacy: What is it? being linked. You are, in essence, friends first and lovers second.

Your marriage is likely to fail if you and your spouse are not friends. You can only go so far in a relationship based on physical attraction.

What will be the most beneficial to you both when the lights go on, things become challenging, and you both need to buckle down and face life together? your companionship.

It is impossible to exaggerate the value of friendship in marriage. Consider what it means to be a friend. You open yourself to one another completely; in fact, you eagerly anticipate speaking to one another. You value the tiny details that make each other unique. Your support and promote one another. That is one amazing relationship!

But doesn't it also seem like it may make for a wonderful union?

What type of friendship can you cultivate in your marriage?

Here are some strategies for strengthening your friendship and making it a bigger part of your married life.

Continue to dream together.

You and your spouse likely discussed your future aspirations when you two first started dating. These aspirations eventually came true when you got married. However, once you get enmeshed in the routine of a family and a job, you often stop talking about your aspirations.

Maybe life is just too busy, or maybe you feel like you can't dream right now because of how demanding it is. Or maybe you believe there is nothing more to say since your spouse already knows about your aspirations. Friends always share dreams. So, even if it has been a while, bring it up with your husband.

Discuss it when you're having supper, traveling, or just relaxing in bed. "Where do you envision yourself and our family in five years?" or "What do you dream about?" or "What are your top three bucket list items?" Maintain them as frequent talking points, and your relationship will continue to develop.

Never doubt your partner.
Consider your childhood best buddy.

Have you ever had any doubts about their ability to carry out their promises? Or have you ever had doubts about their ability to support you?

Friends have each other's backs and can trust one another. When one of them says they're going to train for a marathon, the other should simply believe them and be supportive rather than point out how difficult it will be and cast doubt on their sincerity.

Friends encourage, help, and inspire faith. Friends do things like that, right? When did you last do it for your spouse, by the way?
Your partner is very intelligent. You can rely on them to carefully consider all options and

to act in everyone's best interests. Trust them to act if that is what they want to do. Respect and adore them.

Don't give them a "reality check" to take the wind out of their sails. Because they have likely considered the drawbacks. Stop questioning your husband. Instead, put all of your faith and support in them.

Spend time alone with each other.
Friends usually find a way to hang out together regularly. At least once a week, they hang out together and often text. They often go shopping or attend activities together. But on the weekends, they also do special activities like attending parties, movies, dinners, or other enjoyable events.

To strengthen that friendship link, do the same with your spouse. If all that is happening is that you share a place, you can't genuinely connect. You must go out and engage in a joint activity. Commit to doing it once a week; date night should unquestionably be a requirement of marriage.

Your friendship will soon experience a resurgence of sorts. Place it in your calendar, then follow it through.

Be honest and open

When was the last time you and your partner spoke heart to heart?

Where can you express your emotions and views about something?

Friend do that. They are comfortable with one other's vulnerability, speaking their minds, listening to one another, and just generally sharing. They do it often and sincerely. Because in such moments, two people may feel heard, validated, and connected.

That is the genuine definition of emotional closeness and friendship in marriage—to become one whole as a couple rather than simply two half of a whole. You can do it with the aid of a solid marriage friendship.

The conclusion

One of the cornerstones of a happy marriage is friendship. If you think back to when you and your spouse first met, you probably recall that you two became close as friends before you both experienced romantic attraction. A fantastic and crucial strategy to maintain the relationship's health and happiness is to keep a friendship blossoming during a marriage.

# Chapter 3

The closeness of connections
Relationship intimacy is the sensation of being near, emotionally attached, and supported. It entails being able to communicate a wide variety of human experiences, emotions, and ideas. It entails being honest and open about your feelings and ideas, laying down your guard (being vulnerable), and sharing your aspirations and dreams with another person.

It takes time and works from both couples to develop and sustain intimacy, which takes patience. One of the most satisfying elements of a relationship might be experiencing intimacy with someone you love.

Aside from emotional and sexual intimacy, other types of intimacy include intellectual, recreational, financial, spiritual, artistic (like remodeling your house), crisis-related, and creative closeness (working as a team during tough times).

When we become close to someone and feel comfortable that we are loved and accepted for who we are, we experience intimacy. Children often grow close to their parents and classmates. Adults want closeness in personal friendships, familial interactions, and romantic partnerships.

Sexual intimacy

No matter how satisfying their sexual encounters may be, it is crucial to express a wide variety of feelings with a partner since failing to do so may cause some individuals to feel lonely and alone.

Making love often brings a feeling of intimacy and emotional connection for many couples. It takes trust and openness to be in an intimate sexual relationship. Sexual intimacy and other types of intimacy, such as emotional and spiritual connection, are related. Foreplay and other types of physical intimacy are also an element of sexual intimacy, which goes beyond intercourse.

Remember that sex involves many different types of physical touch and look for methods to express love and affection without having sex. Frequently, a couple's sex relationship gets more rewarding the more intimate they become with one another outside of the sexual activity.

Intimacy creation is difficult

For some couples, developing closeness in their relationship is challenging. Others may observe that once familiarity is attained, it appears to vanish. There are several reasons why some individuals struggle to build closeness in their relationships. This often happens as a consequence of issues like:

Communication problems: If you and your spouse are unable to express your wants and emotions to one another, it is unlikely that they will be satisfied. It is difficult to establish or sustain intimacy if you don't feel understood by your spouse. It's important to communicate your needs to your spouse and to inquire about how they are feeling. It may be difficult to build intimacy in a relationship when there is a constant dispute. This act alone can foster a sense of connection and intimate conflict.

Feeling connected to someone you are disagreeing with is difficult. Intimacy may be harmed by anger, hurt, resentment, distrust, or a feeling of unappreciation. If practical considerations—practical concerns and everyday stresses like financial anxieties, work-related demands, child-related worries, or just being too busy to properly connect—can impair intimacy. It is crucial to attempt to set out a time for your relationship, even if it is only a 5-minute check-in or sharing a cup of tea.

There are times in a relationship when you have to put your needs aside while dealing with more urgent matters. Small acts of intimacy may build up to larger acts of intimacy abuse or violence because intimacy is harmed when one partner waves abuse control over the other. Violence or abuse in a relationship erodes trust and indicates that the union is in peril. It takes time to develop intimacy.

It takes time to develop and maintain intimacy in a relationship, and some individuals require longer than others. The more effort you put into increasing closeness in your relationship, the more gratifying it is often.

The following are some ideas for increasing closeness in your relationship.

Honor the positive aspects of your partnership. Express your love and appreciation for your mate in both words and deeds. Tell your spouse what you like about them and the partnership. Be specific and avoid assuming they are aware of it. Everyone enjoys hearing that they are valued and cherished.

Be honest with one another about your needs in a relationship and your emotions.

Construct intimate settings. Spend time together as a pair when you can give your relationship and each other your full attention. It is much more crucial that you do this the harder it is due to children, employment, or other responsibilities.

Plan a regular evening, day, or weekend when the two of you may be alone yourself.

Recognize that there will be highs and lows in your relationship. Continue to look for novel approaches to achieving more closeness. These exchanges don't have to be elaborate displays of affection. Just as crucial as going on a date is spending time, even little moments, together.

Think positively and express gratitude for your connection.

Be conscious that to build closeness, both people in a relationship must take the initiative.

seeking assistance with relationship issues

You can sometimes require assistance or direction to work through some of the issues, emotions, and ideas you have about your connection. You and your spouse may work through certain relationship issues by speaking with a relationship counselor or attending a program or course.

Intimately touching foreheads, a couple.

Although they may coexist, intimacy and sex are distinct concepts. Find out more about the many forms of intimacy.

Thinkstock

You could presume that "intimacy" refers to sexual connections when you hear the term.

However, although one may help the other, one does not always entail the other. Trust, acceptance and an emotional connection with another person are all prerequisites for intimacy. Sharing ideas wants, and weaknesses is not a problem for intimate couples since they are concerned about one another.

You may have close connections with friends, family, and other individuals in your life in addition to love partners.

Intimacy may help both physical and emotional health even without sexual activity. When no sex is present, individuals nonetheless preserve their paired connection and closeness for evolutionary reasons. Indeed, we have discovered that being a dyad over an individual has physiologic benefits.

Less Stress and Better Sex Are Two of Intimacy's Health Benefits

According to specialists, intimacy provides several physical and mental health advantages. These consist of:

The Benefits of Intimacy on Stress Reduction and Health

Numerous health issues, including sleeplessness, muscular soreness, high blood pressure, cardiac events, a compromised immune system, irritable bowel syndrome, and inflammatory bowel disease, among others, may be brought on by prolonged stress. "You use up a lot of the essential nutrients required to sustain health while you are in a continual state of flight or fight. Intimacy helps your body repair itself and maintain a strong immune system by reducing stress and terror.

Loneliness is countered by intimacy, which also lowers mortality risk.

"Good health is influenced by how liked, valued, and praised you feel. Your health will suffer if you feel depressed, lonely, worried, mistreated, or taken advantage of.

A Better Sexual Life Is Fueled by Intimacy

Although sex is not required to develop closeness, intimacy may often result in a healthier sexual life, which has health advantages of its own. Because you won't be frightened to communicate (and get) what you want, as well as eager and open to hear and care for your partner's needs, your experience of sex will improve. You both will be able to develop and attempt new things thanks to the trust, which may improve your relationship.

9 Organic Ways to Improve Your Sexual Life

According to Krychman, the act of having sex may affect the body in many good ways, including increasing oxytocin, sometimes known as the "cuddle hormone." He continues, "A good sex life may also influence your immune system and blood pressure, alleviate discomfort, and improve sleep." According to Bartlik, an orgasm by itself may lower blood pressure through oxytocin release. She says, "It has a relaxing effect that might last a few days. According to Krychman, having sex is also a sort of exercise, which has numerous positive effects on one's health.

Your mental health may benefit from intimacy.

You also experience an uplift in your mental state when you are intimate with someone. Studies have shown that when intimacy is lacking, males get irate and women become melancholy. When you touch someone, are touched by someone, or share an intimate act like making decisions with someone, your hormone levels—especially oxytocin—actually alter, according to Krychman. "You have more of the joyful chemicals (like dopamine) if you are linked in a loving relationship," he continues.

## Strengthening Forces of Intimacy and Emotional Support

When you are unhappy about something, talking about it with a close, understanding friend or therapist may frequently make you feel better. "You may start to overcome a certain degree of emotional anguish and begin the healing process when you feel supported," Plus, being emotionally insensitive might make you weaker. It might make your sorrow worse and re-traumatize you if you experience someone you trust's lack of empathy or shame. As a result, you may retreat or avoid close interactions, which might worsen your sadness or anxiety."

"The exchange of intimate and private information is a fundamental concept of intimacy. According to this viewpoint, experiencing closeness does not always involve direct face-to-face contact. Even if we are aware that physical contact and other nonverbal indicators play a very important function in fostering greater closeness between people, those who are already acquainted online may still readily utilize the internet for personal exchanges that can support their in-person interactions.

We see this in the context of private text messages we exchange with close friends and family members, where we have a certain style of expressing ourselves with particular people, [certain] words or emoticons that only the other person completely understands. Naturally, being in contact with folks using Skype or Facetime makes it simple to feel more connected to them," she adds.

However, it's crucial to strike a good balance between in-person and online connections. In my view, the internet may be a fantastic tool for fostering intimacy in relationships via a variety of applications, but it most definitely cannot take the place of all forms of human intimacy.

# Chapter 4

The secret to a peaceful and joyful relationship is respect. Healthy social connections, such as those with your family or friends, are just as vital as romantic partnerships.

Some individuals realize the value of respect immediately, while others find it difficult to comprehend why it's crucial to consult partners before making major choices or why we should sometimes swallow our pride and go to the opera with them.

Even if we don't like doing something, we may still do it if we know that it will make our partners feel loved and appreciated.

If one of the partners disrespects the others, even a pleasant relationship might turn sour and jeopardize their future.

How often has someone done something you don't agree with, and you lost respect for them? Or maybe you overheard them talking negatively about you?

Rarely can it be recovered and restored after being lost? In a way, respect is incredibly delicate since it may take a long time to gain and just as quickly be lost.

Describe respect.
What does respect mean to you? Respect for someone is acknowledging their viewpoint, desires, ideas, and emotions as well as loving them and giving them the freedom to be who they are and voice their opinions.

We may respect our spouse in a variety of ways. You must.

- Respect their feelings

You must be sensitive to one another's sentiments. You must respect one another's viewpoints and take care of one another's feelings. To respect emotional values, cooperate, and establish common ground.

Simply acknowledge and appreciate the reality that you and your spouse are two distinct individuals with unique characteristics.

Respect them for who they are

Avoid attempting to alter your spouse or allowing them to change you. If you can't respect them for who they are, you may want to reconsider your relationship.

There will be disagreements but resist the urge to impose your preferences on your spouse.

Recognize that there may be some disagreement between the two of you.

- Be respectful of them as a person.
Respect for your partner's humanity is the absolute prerequisite for respect in a relationship. Please treat your spouse with the same respect you would expect from any other person.

If one of these is lacking, you'll probably find it difficult to resolve this problem in the future, so now could be a good opportunity to talk about how you feel about exhibiting respect in relationships.

The importance of respect in a relationship
There just isn't a strong basis for your future together without it.

Imagine sharing a home with someone who doesn't respect you: they will make choices on their own, even if they affect you as well; they won't treat you well in public, and they will constantly make you feel unimportant and unworthy.

Who would anyone choose to be in such a relationship? You are merely harming your relationship by not exhibiting respect.

If you are with the appropriate spouse, the value of respect between two individuals shouldn't come up as a subject for debate at any time in your life.

However, if you find yourself having to defend the need of treating one another with respect, it suggests that one of you is intellectually challenged.

Even if it might be justified, it can be difficult to deal with when someone treats you disrespectfully.

Even though we may claim to love someone without conditions, when we're struggling, we may behave disrespectfully, which, regrettably, is a reflection of our true feelings.

You undoubtedly know a lot of individuals who are wonderful with money and who believe that purchasing presents, diamonds, or pricey watches are the greatest way to show their lovers how much they love and appreciate them, yet nevertheless, their relationships ended badly or didn't work out.

On the other side, many couples seldom post about their lives on social media, don't purchase expensive jewelry or automobiles, and yet have extremely happy lives. These couples are admired by many people for their happiness.

What causes this to occur? Some individuals don't grasp the value of respect in a relationship, and there are many different methods to demonstrate respect.

Others believe that no respect is required at all. All they need to do is "feel it" and "speak it."

Ten reasons follow why respect in a relationship is crucial:

1. It implies your undying devotion to them. Without respect, there is no such thing as "love," and neither is a fulfilling relationship or marriage.

Why? Because respecting someone in a relationship implies you value and adore them completely. Everything else is only hazy and artificial. A recipe for sorrow is a relationship between two individuals who don't appreciate one another.

2. Respect teaches you to accept others for their shortcomings as well as their qualities. Nobody is flawless, and we only realize this after a few months. When you genuinely respect someone, you will gladly accept both

the good and the bad and work to make them a better person every day by encouraging them and expressing your love and gratitude in both happy and difficult times.

3. You'll develop patience.
Some folks just want everything immediately. Love simply doesn't function this way, which is why these relationships don't last. You must learn to be patient, and you learn to be patient through fostering and developing respect in a relationship.

4. You make better choices.
There will always be certain temptations we must overcome along the path, regardless of how deep the love between two people becomes. You won't be as tempted if respect has been established in a relationship.

Building mutual respect and trust in a relationship is essential because you will always make decisions that are beneficial for both of you rather than just for yourself.

It facilitates communication.
Lack of communication or an incorrect understanding of a partner's emotions, words, or behavior is one of the most frequent causes of breakups and divorces.

Respect in a relationship means that you will always sit down and discuss any issues you are experiencing.

6. You develop an awareness of others.
Egoism has no place in partnerships. Respect for one another motivates altruistic behavior. You put others before yourself and demonstrate love by appreciating their aspirations by assisting them in realizing their full potential.

7. You'll support their success in life
Nothing compares to a partner's words of encouragement. Confidence and self-esteem

may be developed or broken in a relationship through respect.

Your partner's success in life will be influenced by how you treat them. Simply envision yourself in their position and contrast how they fare in life with someone whose voice and wants are completely unheard with someone who feels loved and encouraged.

8. Your sex life will be better if you respect your companion.

There is nothing more enjoyable than sharing passionate moments with a self-assured individual. Why? They do this only if they feel appreciated and loved because they are not hesitant to disclose what they want in bed.

Your relationship will become better overall, and this also applies to your sexual life.

9. Your staunchest ally will be on your side

Being respected by one another in a relationship ensures that each partner has their best ally by their side anytime they need them.

If you respect your spouse, you'll notice that s/he will always have your back. Knowing that the love of your life is always there to support and assist you is a wonderful and comforting feeling.

10. Your partnership will prosper.
If you have discovered someone you truly like, it is important to establish respect in your relationship.

Respect for one another in a relationship ensures that the two of you will go far together and that you will always find a way to get through whatever challenges your union may encounter in the future.

When people respect one another, they are always willing to discuss problems and find solutions.

How can you treat your lover with respect?
Family Hugging

There are a plethora of methods to demonstrate respect in a relationship.

You may focus on forming habits that will strengthen this value in your own life to demonstrate your love and gratitude for them by showing them that you appreciate an essential value they uphold.

Perhaps people donate to charity because they want to assist others. They devote a lot of time and effort to several public causes and provide pro bono labor. You may participate and indicate that you want to assist them. You will have more time together and have the chance to let them know how much you value them.

There are numerous straightforward methods to demonstrate respect in a relationship. Listening is one of the finest ways to demonstrate respect in a relationship.

Give your mate plenty of ear time. They have a strong purpose for disclosing specified information to you. People must understand how attentive you are to what they have to say.

They will seem like a burden if you are not paying attention and are preoccupied with other things, and respectful relationships don't feel like that. You can improve your listening skills, so decide to do so. Your connections will be of far higher caliber as a result.

Respecting others improves your character.

When you learn how to treat others with respect in a relationship, you are also improving yourself as a person.

Selfishness is not a desirable trait in people, and individuals who are only concerned with their own needs, issues, and emotions often find themselves alone and lonely.

The good news is that by treating others with respect regularly, you may enhance your social skills. Everyone will want to be around you, and it will make you gentler and easier to adore.
Respect may be shown for people, concepts, objects, and even our interpersonal connections.
Spend more time, effort, and money on your relationship to nurture it. Ask yourself what you can do to make your life a better and more meaningful journey. Take your travels together. Spend more time with your mate.
Talk to your spouse about the individuals you're seeing who could be putting the two

of you at odds and concentrate on repairing those connections.
Too often, our environments shape who we are, therefore it's critical to consider how you and your partner may modify or enhance the environment in which you both live.

Why are some individuals unable to respect one another?
For some people, relationships and respect go hand in hand, whereas for others, it's difficult to respect one another. They may have been mistreated and feel resentful or abandoned, or they may have come from a dysfunctional household.

People may not appreciate the value of respect for a variety of reasons.

Respect in a relationship may be established if there is a desire to change and evolve, regardless of the cause, including prior relationship trauma or just a lack of basic social skills.

Understanding one another is the foundation for respect in a relationship.

If we don't comprehend someone's background, we can't appreciate them.

Because of this, it's crucial to be patient with your spouse and give them room to speak their mind. Discover their character; the more you know about someone, the more respect you will feel for them.

We are wasting our time and effort attempting to develop a tree from a dead seed if we destroy our connection from the beginning by not allowing them to open up and reveal who they are.

Conclusion

Allow yourself some time to get to know one another and refrain from passing judgment.

Even if we disagree with something they enjoy or do, it doesn't always indicate it's bad.

"Just because you're correct doesn't imply I'm wrong," You may both be correct, which is why respect in a relationship is crucial. You'll discover that there are alternative options and several routes to the same place.

Respect one another and enable your personalities to develop together as a couple. This is the key to a successful, lasting relationship.

# Chapter 5

Even if you're single and actively dating, discussing money isn't necessarily a bad thing.

The question is, how can Americans continue to maintain and develop good relationships while simultaneously working toward their financial objectives, regardless of whether they are married, casually dating, or somewhere in between? Select spoke with two experts on the best ways for individuals to handle their finances and romantic relationships.

How finances and dating interact

It's no secret that individuals in committed relationships often have prosperous financial outcomes.

However, regardless of where you are in the dating process, it is common to be

interested in a possible partner's financial condition if you are actively dating.
In fact, during the pandemic, the probability that a single would state that money matters in a relationship virtually quadrupled. This is probably because many people experienced a lack of financial stability during the early Covid-19-induced shutdowns when unemployment rates soared.

Therefore, in the dating scene, having more money than less is unquestionably a "plus." Unfortunately, the same characteristic that so many people find beautiful may also lead to a relationship's demise. The Institute for Divorce Financial Analysts found that, behind "fundamental incompatibility" and "infidelity," "money concerns" is the third most common reason for divorce. Many couples "lack the communication skills essential to overcome financial issues in their marriage," according to one study respondent.

Why then do so many relationships terminate because of something that is a "plus"?

The psychology of relationships and money
Shared beliefs and the same objectives are prevalent features in great couples, but there is no one secret to relationship success. Hoffman also says that when the topic of personal money comes up, your ambitions and ideals will start to come out organically. Although you and your spouse may not share the same aims and ideals, talking about them may help you get to know each other better and come to agreements on crucial decisions.

Furthermore, these values are developed long before you get your first income.
Anyone's knowledge of and connection with money is dependent on their family of origin as well as any financial literacy training they may acquire throughout their lifetime. It

may be quite diverse from person to person how we think about and comprehend money since we were all taught differently and come from various socioeconomic situations. Rarely do both parties in a love relationship have the same or a comparable financial background. So it's crucial to talk with your significant other, regardless of your background or how difficult it could be.

How to discuss money while you're dating or with a long-term spouse

In any situation, whether dating, asking for a raise at work, or even among friends, talking about money may be challenging.

If your financial condition is not optimal, it may cause you to dread criticism or shame. People may get resentful of you if you are financially literate and love discussing things like your Roth IRA or the newest meme stock. Therefore, have the following in mind before your next financial discussion:

Spend some time getting to know one another's values. For example, if one likes to spend money on dining out while the other chooses to avoid it to save money, there may be a difference in values. Make sure you share your values and the reasons behind them.

Know who is responsible for what costs: Nobody should ever have to guess who is responsible for making a purchase. The ideal moment to determine that is not when the bill arrives or when you are in front of a register, but rather before the problem ever occurs.

Do not impose on others; each person has a unique financial history. And that trip might affect how someone behaves around money and with other people. But no matter what the circumstance, never force your financial beliefs or methods on a partner. It could result in resentment and other problems.

Get "financially naked" if marriage is something you're considering: You may be surprised to learn that one-third of Americans would financially defraud a spouse. Financial infidelity may be just as devastating even if it may not include sexual activity. Therefore, if you're thinking about moving further in your relationship, it's crucial to make sure you discuss any potentially sensitive topics like credit card debt or college debts.

To sum up

It may be challenging to discuss money while dating or in a committed relationship. People believe that talking about politics or religion is simpler than personal economics. The significance of talking about money at any stage of a close relationship. Open and honest communication may work wonders for your present or potential relationship, whether it's discussing investment aspirations with a soon-to-be husband or casually discussing the next hot cryptocurrency coin on a date.

www.ingramcontent.com/pod-product-compliance
Lightning Source LLC
LaVergne TN
LVHW050344160826
845677LV00014B/3785
* 9 7 9 8 8 4 7 2 4 5 0 3 6 *